TAKE ACTION SAVE LIFE ON EARTH

SAVE CARNIVORES

Stephanie Feldstein

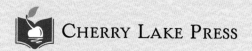

CHERRY LAKE PRESS

Published in the United States of America by Cherry Lake Publishing Group
Ann Arbor, Michigan
www.cherrylakepublishing.com

Reading Adviser: Beth Walker Gambro, MS, Ed., Reading Consultant, Yorkville, IL
Book Designer: Felicia Macheske

Photo Credits: © Anan Kaewkhammul/Shutterstock, cover; © photomaster/Shutterstock, 5, back cover; © Scott E Read/Shutterstock, 9; © miroslav chytil/Shutterstock, 11; © Mircea Costina/Shutterstock, 13; © james_stone76/Shutterstock, 14; © Nina Firsova/Shutterstock, 17; © Kerry Hargrove/Shutterstock, 18; © NDAB Creativity/Shutterstock, 21; © J. Mark Higley 23; © Bob Pool/Shutterstock, 25; © Trevor Clark/Shutterstock, 26; © Rawpixel.com/Shutterstock, 29; © Holly S Cannon/Shutterstock, back cover

Graphics Credits: © Pavel K/Shutterstock; © Panimoni/Shutterstock; © Hulinska Yevheniia/Shutterstock; © Vector Place/Shutterstock; © DianaFinch/Shutterstoc; © Net Vector/Shutterstock; © Mushakesa/Shutterstock; © Peacefully7/Shutterstock

Cherry Lake Press is an imprint of Cherry Lake Publishing Group.

Library of Congress Cataloging-in-Publication Data has been filed and is available at catalog.loc.gov.

Cherry Lake Publishing Group would like to acknowledge the work of the Partnership for 21st Century Learning, a Network of Battelle for Kids. Please visit *http://www.battelleforkids.org/networks/p21* for more information.

Printed in the United States of America
Corporate Graphics

Note from publisher: Websites change regularly, and their future contents are outside of our control. Supervise children when conducting any recommended online searches for extended learning opportunities.

Table of Contents

INTRODUCTION

Carnivores and the Extinction Crisis

Wolf families are called packs. In many ways, they are like human families. They work together to raise their pups. They care for sick or injured pack members. They have best friends.

Wolves are **carnivores**, like polar bears, mountain lions, and coyotes. Carnivores eat other animals to survive.

Many people like carnivores. Others fear them and think they're dangerous. Carnivores don't want to be near people. But many have lost their **habitats**. Habitat is the place where wild animals live. Carnivores have nowhere else to go. Many of them are hunted. Some have been hunted to near **extinction**.

Extinction is when all of one kind of plant or animal die. It affects wild plants and animals. An extinct plant or animal is gone forever. Scientists say we're in an extinction **crisis**. When wildlife goes extinct, it weakens **ecosystems**. Healthy

ecosystems provide food, shelter, water, and clean air. Life on Earth needs all kinds of plants and animals.

Wolves used to roam across most of the United States. Now they're only found in 15 percent of their original habitat. Hundreds of wolves are killed each year. Mountain lions, coyotes, and other carnivores are killed, too.

We can stop the extinction crisis. People like us need to take action. Governments need to act as well. By working together, we can save carnivores.

Why We Need CARNIVORES

Carnivores are at the top of the food chain. They keep the whole ecosystem in balance.

Carnivores eat **omnivores**. Omnivores are animals that eat plants and other animals. But most animals carnivores eat are **herbivores**. Herbivores are animals that survive on plants. When carnivores eat them, it helps keep plants healthy. Those plants are important for streams, rivers, and lakes. They provide shelter for animals. They help fight climate change.

When carnivores disappear, there are too many herbivores. They don't move around as much to find food. They eat too many plants. This changes the ecosystem.

In the 1920s, all the wolves in Yellowstone National Park were killed by hunters. Without wolves, there were too many elk. The elk ate too many willow trees. They stayed by streams and ate young trees. There weren't enough willow trees for beavers to build dams.

Wolves were reintroduced to Yellowstone in 1995. **Reintroduction** is when animals are brought back to a habitat where they once lived. Elk could no longer eat all the trees in one area. Now there are more willow trees for beavers. The beavers build dams that make streams healthier. Fish and birds live in those streams. All these animals need wolves for their habitat.

CHAPTER ONE

Carnivores in the Crosshairs

Humans are the biggest threat to carnivores. People don't usually kill carnivores for their meat. They're killed for their fur. They're also hunted for sport. This is called trophy hunting. People trophy hunt to show they're more powerful than the wild animal. They often display the animals or their skins in their homes. Trophy hunting targets big, rare animals. It can push the animals closer to extinction.

Carnivores are also killed for preying on livestock. If one cow or sheep is eaten by a wolf or coyote, the entire pack may be killed. Scientists say this doesn't make the cattle or sheep any safer. It makes the ecosystem less healthy. But many ranchers see carnivores as the enemy.

Mountain lions are carnivores that are hunted for sport, to protect livestock or pets, and rarely, for public safety.

TURNING POINT

Tigers were first brought to the United States in the 1800s. They were used in traveling circuses. They were kept in zoos. They were very popular attractions. By the 1970s, some wealthy people wanted their own tigers. It became easy to buy and sell tigers.

Today, more tigers are kept in cages in the United States than are left in the wild. But it's dangerous to keep tigers as pets. It's cruel to keep them in cages.

A law was passed in 2003 to stop the sale of tigers and other big cats. But people kept breeding and selling them. Animal protection groups tried for years to make the law stronger. It finally happened after a Netflix TV series came out in 2020.

Tiger King was about a man who used tigers to make money. His tigers were abused and killed. People got hurt, too. U.S. legislators realized the law needed to

Tigers need a lot of space to hunt. Habitat loss and conflicts with humans mean there are very few left in the wild.

change. They passed the **Big Cat Public Safety Act** in 2022. It makes it illegal for people to own big cats like tigers, lions, and leopards. It protects the animals from abuse. It helps draw attention to the need to protect big cats in the wild.

More than 90 million cattle are raised in the United States each year. They need a lot of space to graze. Cattle don't just eat grass. They also eat crops like corn, soybeans, and hay. Most pigs and chickens raised for meat are kept indoors. But they need a lot of food, too. Grazing and growing crops for animals takes up a huge amount of space. It uses 80 percent of all U.S. farmland. That's as big as almost half the country. That land used to be habitat for carnivores and other wildlife.

Carnivore habitat is also paved over to build towns and roads. Florida panthers and mountain lions are hit by cars every year when trying to cross roads.

Words can harm animals. People often talk about carnivores like they're villains. They're called "pests." Carnivores are seen as mean and dangerous. They're the Big Bad Wolf in fairy tales. When people talk about carnivores this way, other people don't care about them as much. They ignore the ways they help ecosystems. It's easier to make excuses to kill them.

We can stop seeing carnivores as villains. Talking about the importance of carnivores can help people be less afraid. Seeing carnivores as good makes it easier to protect them.

Climate change is another threat to carnivores. Warmer temperatures melt the sea ice that polar bears need to hunt. Climate change also harms the animals that carnivores eat.

It's becoming harder for carnivores to find enough to eat. They have to look for food near ranches and neighborhoods. This can cause **human-wildlife conflict**. That's when people and wild animals come into contact with each other with negative results. Sometimes people get hurt. But often it's something small, like coyotes digging through trash. The animal may be moved away from people. But more often, carnivores are killed after conflicts.

◀ Warmer ocean temperatures melt sea ice that polar bears and other cold climate animals need to move around on. Without the ice, they cannot hunt.

CHAPTER TWO

Take Extinction Off Your Plate

The meat industry causes many of the threats carnivores face. The more meat people eat, the bigger the industry grows. That makes it harder for carnivores to survive.

The food on our plates can help or harm carnivores. We wouldn't need as much space to raise animals if people ate less meat. Less land used for ranching would leave more room for carnivores.

Growing crops like vegetables, grains, and beans takes much less space than raising animals for meat. These **plant-based foods** cause less harm to the environment. They're also an important part of a healthy diet.

Plant-based burgers are a tasty option if you want to eat less meat.

The **Endangered Species** Act is a U.S. law passed to help wildlife. Endangered species are plants and animals in danger of extinction. The law says the government has to protect them and their habitat. This protection gives them a chance to survive. But it only works if the government agrees that the plants and animals need protection.

Many carnivores are protected by the Endangered Species Act. Others need protection but don't have it yet.

You probably already eat a lot of plant-based foods. Vegetables, pasta, rice, beans, nuts, and fruit are all plant-based. Lots of plants have protein. Eating more plant-based foods and less meat helps carnivores.

It's not always easy to change what we eat. But you don't have to change everything at once to make a difference. You don't have to give up your favorite foods. You can try taking small steps to eat less meat. Start with the meat dishes you won't miss as much. Think about foods that are easy to replace. Put beans in tacos instead of beef. Have vegetarian chili or sloppy joes. Try plant-based versions of burgers and chicken nuggets.

You can also eat less meat by eating more plants. Fill your plate with healthy fruits and vegetables. Leave just a small space for meat. Think of it as a side dish instead of a main course. You can pick a meal or a day to eat meat-free. You can join the Meatless Monday movement. Or you can make breakfast or lunch your daily meal to help carnivores.

Try new things. Many delicious meat-free dishes are available. There may be foods and flavors you've never tried before. They might become your new favorites. Ask your family to taste-test new recipes with you. Tell them why meat-free recipes help carnivores.

Talk to your family about making some days ▶ meatless. It can be fun to try new meat-free dishes, and you will help carnivores, too.

CONSERVATION CHAMPION

The Hoopa Valley Tribe lives in Northern California. They lived there long before California was a state. One of the animals they share the land with is the fisher. Fishers are an important part of their tribal culture.

Fishers are small carnivores who live in forests. They're about the size of a house cat. They eat birds, small animals, and fruit. People used to trap fishers for their fur. Their habitat has been destroyed by people cutting down trees.

Hoopa Valley Tribe members know a lot about fishers. Hidden cameras help them see what fishers are doing. Radio collars help them see where the animals go. They track how many fishers live in the area. They study their behavior. They learn where the fishers prefer to live. Then they know what areas to protect from people cutting down trees.

The information collected by the tribe helps **conservation**. Conservation is action to protect wildlife and nature. We need to understand wildlife like fishers to know how to protect them. The fishers also help people understand the whole ecosystem. If fishers are sick or hungry, other animals might be in trouble, too.

Hoopa Valley Tribal member, Aaron Pole, holds a fisher kit (baby) and gets ready to send it back up into a tree.

CHAPTER THREE

Living Alongside Carnivores

Producing less meat will leave more room for carnivores. But we also need to learn to live alongside each other. This is called **coexistence**.

Ranchers who coexist with carnivores agree not to kill them. They're careful not to make their livestock easy prey. They use range riders. Range riders are people on horses who keep an eye on grazing cattle. Wolves and coyotes are more likely to stay away when people are around.

Some ranchers coexist with carnivores by keeping their cattle close together and where they can be watched.

Coyotes get in trouble for stealing food from people. They dig in trash cans. They eat pet food left on porches. Sometimes they kill pets that are outdoors. Many people get scared when they see or hear coyotes. But the coyotes were there first. We moved into their neighborhood.

Coyotes live in almost every city in the United States. But they like to stay hidden. It's safer for everyone if they stay away from people. Don't leave pets outdoors by themselves. Don't leave pet food or trash outside. It's up to us to prevent human-wildlife conflict.

Ranchers can help prevent conflict. They use stronger fences to keep their livestock safe. They install flashing lights near pens. The lights make it look like people are moving around. Motion sensors detect when an animal is near. They sound an alarm or flash a light. Some ranchers have dogs to scare away carnivores. Others have llamas to protect sheep or goats. Llamas are fierce defenders of smaller animals.

Ranchers have seen carnivores as the enemy for a long time. They can learn new ways to live with them. They need to see that coexistence works. Local governments and organizations have programs to help. They pay for things like fencing and dogs. They teach ranchers how to keep carnivores away.

Marin County in California has a coexistence program. It helped reduce the number of cattle killed by carnivores. Most ranchers liked the new program better than the old way of killing any nearby carnivores.

SPEAK UP FOR CARNIVORES

Coexistence isn't just for ranchers. Coyotes have learned to live near humans. They've become part of the ecosystems in towns and cities. They stay hidden most of the time. But sometimes they stop being afraid of people. Then conflicts can happen.

Project Coyote teaches people to coexist with coyotes. They have a program called Coyote Friendly Communities. They help people appreciate coyotes. They teach them how to prevent conflicts.

Project Coyote's website has flyers with coyote facts. They give tips on how to coexist. You can download these flyers to share with friends and neighbors. You can also make your own flyers. Research facts about coyotes. Read about how coyotes and people can coexist. Write down three to five fun facts and safety tips. Ask if you

Ask if you can post a Project Coyote flyer at your school or at a business in your neighborhood.

can post your flyer at school. Look for bulletin boards at parks or coffee shops where you can post it, too.

Ask your town to become a Coyote Friendly Community. Town leaders can post Project Coyote's signs in parks. Project Coyote can help educate officials on how to help coyotes. Send your mayor or town council a letter. Tell them about Coyote Friendly Communities and ask them to join.

CREATE A CARNIVORE-FRIENDLY CAFETERIA

School cafeterias have a huge impact on the planet. Billions of meals are served in schools every year. Most of them are meat dishes like hot dogs and chicken nuggets. These foods increase threats to carnivores.

Here's how you can ask your school to change its menu:

1 Write a letter to your principal asking for more plant-based choices in the cafeteria. Tell them how plant-based foods help wild animals. They're also better for the climate and your health.

2 Ask your teacher if you can talk about your letter in class. Tell your classmates about how to help carnivores. Then ask your friends to sign the letter with you. Parents can sign, too. More signatures show that lots of people want better school meals.

3 Ask your principal if you can meet with the person in charge of cafeteria food to share ideas. Use the ideas in Chapter 2 to talk about how to start slow. Your school can try Meatless Mondays or offer meat as a side dish.

4 Tell the cafeteria workers what kinds of plant-based meals you think will be popular. Some schools serve dishes like veggie fried rice, chili, and lasagna. Your cafeteria can have taste tests for new recipes. These tests will help them learn which meals students like.

Celebrate if your school agrees to try more plant-based meals. But your work isn't done. You can help make sure it's a success. Let the cafeteria staff know what you like. Ask your friends to try the new dishes.

LEARN MORE

Castaldo, Nancy F. *Back from the Brink: Saving Animals from Extinction*. New York, NY: Clarion Books, 2022.

Isabella, Jude. *Bringing Back the Wolves: How a Predator Restored an Ecosystem*. Toronto, ON: Kids Can Press, 2020.

Musick, Barb. *The Vegan Cookbook for Kids*. Emeryville, CA: Rockridge Press, 2020.

Viola, Jason. *Polar Bears: Survival on the Ice*. New York, NY: First Second, 2019.

GLOSSARY

carnivores (KAHR-nuh-vohrz) animals that eat other animals to survive

coexistence (koh-ihg-ZIH-stuhns) when animals and people live alongside each other in peace

conservation (kahn-suhr-VAY-shuhn) action to protect wildlife and nature

crisis (KRY-suhss) a very difficult time or emergency

ecosystems (EE-koh-sih-stuhmz) places where plants, animals, and the environment rely on each other

endangered species (in-DAYN-juhrd SPEE-sheez) plants and animals in danger of extinction

extinction (ik-STINK-shuhn) when all of one kind of plant or animal die

habitats (hah-BUH-tatz) the natural homes of plants and animals

herbivores (HURH-buh-vohrz) animals that eat plants to survive

human-wildlife conflict (HYOO-muhn-WYLD-lyfe KAHN-flikt) when people and wildlife come into contact with negative results

omnivores (AHM-nuh-vohrz) animals that eat both plants and other animals

plant-based foods (PLAHNT-BAYST FOODZ) foods made from plants like vegetables, pasta, rice, beans, nuts, and fruit

reintroduction (ree-ihn-truh-DUHK-shuhn) when plants or animals are brought back to the habitat where they once lived

INDEX